TWO TENEBRAE READINGS AND SERVICES

Richard A. Dinges

CSS Publishing Company, Inc., Lima, Ohio

TWO TENEBRAE READINGS AND SERVICES

Copyright © 1997 by
CSS Publishing Company, Inc.
Lima, Ohio

ISBN: 0-7880-0757-2   PRINTED IN U.S.A.

This book is dedicated to all those readers who presented these services at Lynnfield Community Church, UCC, Lynnfield, Massachusetts, and St. John's United Church of Christ, Wheeling, West Virginia.

Table of Contents

Introduction

This booklet contains two Tenebrae services, each with an accompanying order of worship. The first Tenebrae service contains nine readers' parts, including the Narrator. The second Tenebrae service assigns scriptural readings for twelve readers; however, parts could be doubled up if fewer readers are available.

Readers can be recruited during the week prior to the service. A short rehearsal an hour before the service is needed. Someone with a flair for drama can help the readers make it come alive. For example, the man with the formerly withered hand can raise a good hand as he introduces himself. After rehearsal, the readers take their seats among the congregation.

Setup includes two long church tables at the front of the sanctuary. Arrange as many chairs as you have readers behind the tables and facing the congregation.

Place a candle-holder and short candle for each reader on the tables by each chair. (The short candle allows the light of the candle to be closer to the text.) Also needed are a portable microphone, matches, and a candle-snuffer.

The bread and cup can be placed at the center of the tables for the celebration of the Lord's supper by intinction. The elements can remain there for the duration of the Tenebrae.

The candlesticks and offering plates are removed from the altar. The ushers keep the plates in back. There should be no flowers. All that is to be on the altar are the cross and the Christ candle (the large candle often used for the center of the Advent wreath). This candle is not lighted until the end of the service.

Conducting The Tenebrae: Persons who have reading parts should come forward during the last hymn. They should sit in the order in which they will read. At the same time, the choir, if there is a choir, may come down to sit with the congregation. Then the candles are lighted, the sanctuary lights are extinguished, and the narrator begins.

Each reader speaks slowly and distinctly into the microphone. Eye contact with the congregation is not needed. Readers should keep their eyes on their parts. After each reader is done, his or her candle is extinguished, and the snuffer is passed along to the next reader. All the readers remain seated until the end of the service.

After the readers have finished, the congregation should remain in the total darkness for several minutes. Then someone should lead the Lord's Prayer. This is a good introduction: "And now let us pray together as Jesus taught his disciples, saying 'Our Father....' "

Finally, someone lights the Christ candle. After a minute or two an usher should light the narthex so people can leave without tripping. Worshippers may linger and then leave in silence.

Bulletin Information: The following information could be included in your worship bulletin with either Tenebrae service.

The Service Of The Tenebrae: This service is an adaptation of an early fourth century office traditionally sung during Holy Week. The gradual extinguishing of the candles is symbolic of the flight of the disciples, the approach of the dark hatred of Jesus' enemies, and the resentment of the world, leading to the final isolation of Jesus on the cross. The moment of darkness recalls the hours of death's despair and hopelessness. The lighting of the Christ candle points ahead to the Easter soon to dawn.

Tenebrae I

Order Of Service

Organ Prelude

Call To Worship

Minister: The Christ said, "This is my commandment: Love one another."

People: **We come to worship the God who is love, that we may learn to love one another.**

Minister: The Christ said, "No longer do I call you servants, but now I call you my friends."

People: **We come to worship the God whose friends we are through Christ.**

All: **Let us sing praise to God and live in love and friendship toward the human family, through Jesus our Christ. Amen.**

Invocation

Hymn   "O Sacred Head, Now Wounded"

Unison Reading

Scripture   John 15:12-17

Special Music

Pastoral Prayer

Hymn   "What A Friend We Have In Jesus"

Sermon

Offering

Offertory Prayer

The Lord's Supper

Hymn   "Let All Mortal Flesh Keep Silence"

The Service Of The Tenebrae

(You are asked to depart from this service in silence.)

Tenebrae Reading

Narrator

Thank you for coming to this hastily-called meeting of the followers of Jesus. As you probably have heard, Jesus has been arrested. We heard that Judas Iscariot, one of his disciples, betrayed his location to the authorities. Currently Jesus is being held by the Roman guard. We believe false charges will be brought against him. We don't know what we can do to gain his freedom, but we want to hear from those who experienced God's salvation through him. Many of them have gathered here to tell their stories.

Peter's Mother-in-law   (Luke 4:38ff)

I am the mother-in-law of Peter. I am one of Jesus' disciples. I became Jesus' disciple after he cured me of a high fever. It was on the day that Jesus first came to my house. I didn't want Peter to bring anyone home that day. The house was a mess. But Peter just had to bring him so I could meet him. Peter had been telling me so much about Jesus. On that day I was sick in bed. I had been ill for many days. I wasn't expecting company. When I saw company coming into my house I felt embarrassed and inadequate. Beside the house being a mess, I couldn't get up and show common hospitality.

Then a marvel took place I will never forget. Jesus stood at my bedside and prayed. Suddenly I felt well. How it happened, I don't know. But immediately I got up and began serving them, and I have been a disciple of Jesus ever since.

Formerly Paralyzed Man *(walks in)*   (Luke 5:17-26)

I too am Jesus' disciple. One day Jesus figured importantly in my life also. I was paralyzed. I had been lying on my stretcher in that condition for a long time. Then Jesus came to town. Before I knew it, four men were picking me up to take me to the house where Jesus was teaching. Too many people were crowded around the house for us to get close. So these men lifted me up to the roof of the house, took the roof apart, and lowered me into Jesus' presence. I couldn't say anything. I was afraid I would be blamed for the damage to the roof — but nobody said anything — until Jesus said, "Friend, your sins are forgiven." I just waited there, and the guys were looking down through the hole in the roof, and then Jesus said, "Take up your stretcher and go home." And that's exactly what I did — and I have been following Jesus — literally — ever since.

Man With Formerly Withered Hand (raises hand before speaking)   (Luke 6:6-10)
    Me next! Let me tell my story. I met Jesus in the synagogue. I used to be employed as a carpenter, but I became disabled. I injured my hand and it became useless. After that I felt like an outcast. I couldn't work. I couldn't support my family. So I began spending a lot of time at the synagogue praying. I prayed that God would help me.
    One Sabbath day I was in the synagogue and Jesus came in. The religious leaders were watching him to see if he would do any work on that day. I heard them talking about it. Jesus saw me shortly after he entered the synagogue. He looked around and also saw the icy stares of the scribes and the Pharisees. Then he spoke right up. He said to me, "Arise and come forward." He told me to stretch out my hand, and as I did, it was completely restored — see?

Widow Of Nain *(wearing black veil)*   (Luke 7:11-17)
    The day of my son's funeral was the saddest — and the happiest — day of my life. I was already a widow of five years. My son had been my only support. But he became terribly ill, and then he died. I felt condemned by God to poverty and grief for the rest of my life. The day of the funeral, Jesus and his disciples visited our town of Nain. I saw them as our procession was moving to the cemetery. I never expected what happened next. Jesus stopped our procession. He went over to the coffin and touched it. He said, "Young man, I say to you, arise!" My son — who was dead — sat

up and started talking. Jesus helped him out of the coffin, and led him back to me. I still can't believe it!

Former Sinner Woman (Luke 7:36-50)

I never cared what people thought of me — until I met Jesus. What he told me helped me believe that I was worth something. I was really feeling bad about my life. Then I heard that Jesus was coming to town. I really wanted to meet him. I felt drawn to him. I heard he helped people like me.

I found him at a dinner at a Pharisee's house. I went in and stood near Jesus while he was reclining at the table. I guess I was weeping a lot because my tears wet Jesus' feet. Then I don't know what came over me. I knelt down and began wiping his feet with my hair. I kissed his feet and anointed them with my own perfume.

When I looked up, Jesus was looking at me. He said, "Your sins have been forgiven. Your faith has saved you. Go in peace."

Former Demoniac *(dressed in a nice suit)* (Luke 8:26ff)

I used to live in hell — or hell used to live in me. I am the man from the territory of the Gadarenes. I used to live in tombs. I used to run around naked and scare people. Everyone left me alone, except when they would come as a group and try to bind me with chains. But I would always break free and run away.

One day I was wandering by the sea and I saw a man coming toward me. No person dared come to me alone. So I was taken with the sight of him. He came right up to me and asked, "What is your name?" A voice came out of my mouth. "Legion," it said, "for we are many." After that all I remember is watching all the swine run down the hill and into the lake.

I wanted to start following Jesus right away — as soon as I got some clothes on, but Jesus told me to go back to my home first. Now all my family are followers of Jesus.

Samaritan Woman *(wearing a colored shawl)* (John 4:3ff)

You wouldn't expect Jesus, a Jew, to speak to a Samaritan, let alone to a Samaritan woman, but that's just what happened. Jesus spoke to me at Jacob's well. I had come to get water for ... for my friend and myself, and Jesus asked me if I would draw some for him, too. I was surprised that Jesus would say anything to me, the way Jews feel about Samaritans. I didn't see any reason why I shouldn't answer him, or why I shouldn't give him a drink. What amazed me was that Jesus knew all about my past husbands — and my friend. He knew that he was not my husband.

Jesus also knew my heart. For a long time I have been searching for God, and for a right heart before God. Jesus said he would give me living water if only I would ask. I did ask, and I have been a worshipper of God — the living God — ever since.

Boy Who Had Loaves And Fishes (John 6:1-14)

One day years ago my mom packed my lunch and I went fishing. I didn't catch anything all day. I was hungry, so I was about to eat my lunch when I caught sight of a huge crowd of people coming in my direction. I joined the crowd, and found they were following Jesus. Before long someone asked me to bring my lunch to Jesus. I had five small barley loaves and two small fishes. I was hungry, but I felt special to be asked to give my lunch to Jesus. Guess what happened? Jesus took my lunch and blessed it. He gave it to the crowd. He gave it and kept on giving it. I never saw so much food! There must have been 5,000 men, not to mention women and children, in that crowd. They all ate till they were full. And there were twelve baskets full of food left over. Then Jesus thanked me — can you imagine?

We don't know what will happen with Jesus, but we hope that he will be set free so we can be with him again.

Tenebrae II

Order Of Service

Organ Prelude

Call To Worship

Minister: Come to Gethsemane, where Jesus prayed and was betrayed. Come to the courts of justice, to Pilate, where the Righteous One was found guilty.

People: **Come to the hill outside Jerusalem, where the Innocent One suffered and died. Come let us bow down in awe, for what happened there was done for us.**

Unison Invocation

Grant us, O Lord, in all our ways of life, thy help in all our perplexities of thought, thy counsel in all our dangers of temptation, thy protection in all our sorrows of heart. Sanctify us that out of the darkness of thy mystery there may grow a deeper wisdom within us, that out of its shadows may grow our faith for today and our hope for tomorrow, through Jesus Christ our Lord. Amen.

Hymn   "The Old Rugged Cross"

Unison Reading

Scripture   Hebrews 9:11-28

Special Music

Pastoral Prayer

Hymn   "In The Cross Of Christ I Glory"

Sermon

Offertory

Offertory Prayer

The Lord's Supper

Hymn   "My Jesus, I Love Thee"

The Service Of The Tenebrae

(You are asked to depart from this service in silence.)

Tenebrae Reading

Narrator

Tonight we are asked to remember all that Jesus suffered for us. Our Lord gave himself for us. He had reigned with God, and was our God, but was willing to become a man, to become a human savior. As a man he served God obediently without fault as humankind was meant to do. In this he showed that the human race could be redeemed. In his life he loved and obeyed God, even to death on a cross. For our sakes he was consumed as bread and poured out like wine. His death provided a sacrifice for the sins of all who would seek to be forgiven in his name.

Reader 1

Jesus said, "I am the light of the world." He came into this world so that sinful humankind might have life, and might have it abundantly. But men loved darkness rather than light because their deeds were evil.

Reader 2

When his time was at hand, knowing the course that lay before him, Jesus set his face firmly toward Jerusalem, the place of the martyrdom of all the prophets.

"As the time approached for him to be taken up to heaven, Jesus resolutely set out for Jerusalem" (Luke 9:51). He knew God's purposes for himself, and he anguished. He said, "I have a baptism to undergo, and how distressed I am until it is completed!" (Luke 12:50).

Reader 3

On his way to Jerusalem, Jesus was bereft of anyone who could understand his grief.

"Jesus took the Twelve aside and told them, 'We are going up to Jerusalem, and everything that is written by the prophets about the Son of Man will be fulfilled. He will be handed over to the

Gentiles. They will mock him, insult him, spit on him, flog him and kill him. On the third day he will rise again.' The disciples did not understand any of this. Its meaning was hidden from them, and they did not know what he was talking about" (Luke 18:31-34).

Reader 4

Jesus' disciples were sure of their commitment to him, but he foretold their abandonment of him. He said, "A time is coming, and has come, when you will be scattered, each to his own home. You will leave me all alone. Yet I am not alone, for my father is with me" (John 16:32).

For fear of suffering with him, we, too, would probably have abandoned him.

Peter was the boldest, that rough-hewn rock, Peter. He declared his loyalty to the Christ. He said, "Lord, I am ready to go with you to prison and to death." But Jesus replied, "I tell you, Peter, before the rooster crows today, you will deny three times that you know me" (Luke 22:33, 34).

Reader 5

Even in his darkest hour, his disciples could not stay awake and watch with him. "Jesus went with his disciples to a place called Gethsemane, and he said to them, 'Sit here while I go over there and pray.' He took Peter and the two sons of Zebedee along with him, and he began to be sorrowful and troubled. Then he said to them, 'My soul is overwhelmed with sorrow to the point of death. Stay here and keep watch with me.' Going a little farther, he fell with his face to the ground and prayed, 'My Father, if it is possible, may this cup be taken from me. Yet not as I will, but as you will.' Then he returned to his disciples and found them sleeping. 'Could you men not keep watch with me for one hour?' he asked Peter. 'Watch and pray so that you will not fall into temptation. The spirit is willing, but the body is weak.' He went away a second time and prayed, 'My Father, if it is not possible for this cup to be taken away unless I drink it, may your will be done.' When he came back, he again found them sleeping, because their eyes were heavy. So he left them and went away once more and prayed the third time, saying the same thing. Then he returned to the disciples and said to them, 'Are you still sleeping and resting? Look, the hour is near, and the Son of Man is betrayed into the hands of sinners' " (Matthew 26:36-45).

Reader 6

A friend betrayed him by revealing his location and identity to the authorities. "While he was still speaking, Judas, one of the Twelve, arrived. With him was a large crowd armed with swords and clubs, sent from the chief priests and the elders of the people. Now the betrayer had arranged a signal with them: 'The one I kiss is the man: Arrest him.' Going at once to Jesus, Judas said, 'Greetings, Rabbi!' And kissed him" (Matthew 26:47-49).

"Jesus, knowing all that was going to happen to him, went out and asked them, 'Who is it you want?' 'Jesus of Nazareth,' they replied. 'I am he,' Jesus said. (And Judas the traitor was standing there with them.) When Jesus said, 'I am he,' they drew back and fell to the ground. Again he asked them, 'Who is it you want?' And they said, 'Jesus of Nazareth.' 'I told you that I am he,' Jesus answered. 'If you are looking for me, then let these men go' " (John 18:4-8).

Reader 7

"Then Jesus said to the chief priests, the officers of the Temple guard, and the elders who had come for him. 'Am I leading a rebellion, that you have come with swords and clubs? Every day I was with you in the Temple courts, and you did not lay a hand on me. But this is your hour — when darkness reigns' " (Luke 22:52, 53).

"Then the detachment of soldiers with its commander and the Jewish officials arrested Jesus. They bound him and brought him first to Annas, who was with the father-in-law of Caiaphas, the high priest that year. Caiaphas was the one who had advised the Jews that it would be good if one man died for the people" (John 18:12-14).

Reader 8

"The chief priests and the whole Sanhedrin were looking for evidence against Jesus so that they could put him to death, but they did not find any. Many testified falsely against him, but their statements did not agree. Then some stood up and gave this false testimony against him: 'We heard him say, "I will destroy this manmade temple and in three days will build another, not made by man." ' Yet even then their testimony did not agree. Then the high priest stood up before them and asked Jesus, 'Are you not going to answer? What is this testimony that these men are bringing against you?' But Jesus remained silent and gave no answer" (Mark 14:55-61a). Jesus would not speak to remove the cross which was his to bear. He did not even ask for God's deliverance because he knew the purpose for which he had come into this world.

"As Simon Peter stood warming himself, he was asked, 'Aren't you one of his disciples?' He denied it, saying, 'I am not' " (John 18:25). Peter denied twice more, and immediately a rooster began to crow.

Reader 9

"The men who were guarding Jesus began mocking and beating him. They blindfolded him and demanded, 'Prophesy! Who hit you?' And they said many other insulting things to him" (Luke 22:63-65).

"Then Pilate took Jesus and had him flogged. The soldiers twisted together a crown of thorns and put it on his head. They clothed him in a purple robe and went up to him again and again, saying, 'Hail, O King of the Jews!' And they struck him in the face" (John 19:1-3).

Reader 10

"Early in the morning, all the chief priests and the elders of the people came to the decision to put Jesus to death" (Matthew 27:1). He was brought before Pilate, then Herod, then back to Pilate, but no one would stand up for him.

Reader 11

At last the people demanded that he be crucified. " 'Why? What crime has he committed?' asked Pilate. But they shouted all the louder, 'Crucify him!' " (Mark 15:14).

"Finally, Pilate handed him over to them to be crucified" (John 19:16).

Reader 12

"As they led him away, they seized Simon from Cyrene, who was on his way in from the country, and put the cross on him and made him carry it behind Jesus" (Luke 23:26).

"When they came to the place called The Skull, there they crucified him, along with the criminals — one on his right, the other on his left. Jesus said, 'Father, forgive them for they do no know what they are doing.' And they divided up his clothes by casting lots" (Luke 23:33-35).

"It was now about the sixth hour, and darkness came over the whole land until the ninth hour, for the sun stopped shining" (Luke 23:44, 45a).

www.ingramcontent.com/pod-product-compliance
Lightning Source LLC
Chambersburg PA
CBHW071813020426
42331CB00008B/2482